Fun With Spelling

by Lynne Bradbury
illustrated by Sara Sliwinska

Ladybird Books

Spelling aids

The best way of learning to spell words, or to practise words you find difficult, is like this:

LOOK	SAY	COVER	WRITE	CHECK
at the word.	the word.	the word with a strip of paper.	the word.	to see if it's correct!

Make your own special 'covering strip' from card or paper and use it each time you practise spelling.

Sara   Tom

Write your name on it and add a pattern, picture or message.

WORD once	Try 1 onse Check X	Try 2 once Check ✓	Try 3 Check___	Try 4 Check___

Make a strip, like the one above, for practising a word you find hard to spell.
Fold the word panel underneath when you make your first try. Fold it back to check your answer. If it's wrong, try again.

Make your own dictionary. Use a long thin notebook and label the pages from **a** to **z**. Write words you find hard under the correct letter.

Use a real dictionary to check unusual spellings and to find out the meanings of new words.

Have a go!

Practise using **LOOK**, **SAY**, **COVER**, **WRITE**, **CHECK** with these common nouns. On this page there are pictures to help you.

USE	LOOK	SAY	COVER	WRITE	CHECK

book		_____		☐
watch		_____		☐
money		_____		☐
aeroplane		_____		☐
house		_____		☐
shoes		_____		☐
telephone		_____		☐
pencil		_____		☐
bicycle		_____		☐
present		_____		☐

DID YOU GET THEM ALL RIGHT FIRST TIME?

Magic 'e'

Lots of little words become new words when **e** is added. The **e** changes the sound of the vowel (a, e, i, o, u) that comes earlier in the word.

pin becomes pine   tap becomes tape

Now try these.

add 'e'   COVER   WRITE   CHECK

mat	_____	_____	☐
hop	_____	_____	☐
pip	_____	_____	☐
cap	_____	_____	☐
not	_____	_____	☐
slid	_____	_____	☐
mad	_____	_____	☐

Verbs which end in an 'e' lose the 'e' when you add 'ing'

Like these:

hope → hoping   make → making

Try these:

ride _____   love _____

hide _____   hate _____

Find the little words

Many longer words contain a smaller word.
Underline the small word then write the whole word again.

ear

beard _____   clear   _____

learn _____   heart   _____

fear _____   search   _____

arm

farm _____   alarm   _____

warm _____   armour   _____

harm _____   charm   _____

ail

snail _____   trail   _____

fail _____   nail   _____

rail _____   sailing   _____

 LOOK OUT FOR...

Make your own lists for each one.

Letter patterns

Many words contain the same pattern
of letters either at the beginning of the word, in the middle or
at the end.

 Practise these using:

LOOK	SAY	COVER	WRITE	CHECK

Then add more to each list and write them in your dictionary.

ch

chair _____

child _____

chin _____

str

street _____

straight _____

strong _____

ai

again _____

pain _____

explain _____

ou

thought _____

mouth _____

house _____

dge

badge _____

lodge _____

porridge _____

ck

lick _____

stick _____

back _____

Sounds alike!

Some words have letter patterns that sound the same but are spelt differently.

Here are some to practise – add your own.

ee and ea

feet _____
meat _____
sweet _____
speak _____
_____
_____

f and ph

farm _____
photo _____
flake _____
phone _____
_____

ite and ight

spite _____
light _____
kite _____
fight _____
_____
_____

ow and oa

crow _____
boat _____
follow _____
coat _____
_____

Adjectives

Adjectives describe something. They tell us more about things and make our language more interesting.

Look at the treasure chest and write out the adjective that goes with each noun in the list below.

starry

brave

sour

funny

pretty

fierce

sharp

stolen

clever

tall

interesting

mechanical

1 _____ tiger

2 _____ lemon

3 _____ soldier

4 _____ book

5 _____ girl

6 _____ toy

7 _____ night

8 _____ scientist

9 _____ jewels

10 _____ building

11 _____ clown

12 _____ knife

What a noise!

Choose a word from the bubble below that you think best describes the noise made by each animal.

Write the words again in your dictionary.

1	sheep	_____
2	frogs	_____
3	birds	_____
4	snakes	_____
5	monkeys	_____
6	horses	_____

7	cows	_____
8	geese	_____
9	wolves	_____
10	lions	_____
11	owls	_____
12	elephants	_____

hoot   hiss   sing

moo   baa   cackle   chatter

howl

roar   trumpet   neigh

croak

Looks the same

One of the hardest things in the English language, especially for a foreigner, is the number of words that look the same but are said (**pronounced**) differently.

Practise these:

Ask a grown up to check the way you say each word!

ough

cough   _____

dough   _____

bough   _____

through   _____

bought   _____

ow

row   _____

bow   _____

owl   _____

bowl   _____

Can you think of some more words like these?

_____

10

Opposites

Find the word in the word search which is the **opposite** of each word below. You can go backwards, forwards, up, down or diagonally.

1 up _____

2 out _____

3 first _____

4 wet _____

5 happy _____

6 right _____

7 old _____

8 noisy _____

9 fast _____

10 front _____

11 yes _____

12 day _____

c	d	e	a	l	m	q	n	o
n	i	g	h	t	v	u	n	t
s	q	r	w	i	s	i	e	z
v	d	o	w	n	p	e	w	n
x	r	d	c	r	s	t	u	o
t	y	l	z	b	f	c	g	j
d	h	o	k	t	l	e	f	t
m	v	r	y	z	s	a	d	x
s	l	o	w	g	f	e	s	u
h	i	b	a	c	k	j	k	t

happy

left

slow

1ST

Write the words again in your dictionary!

11

Easy crosswords

Clues down

SHAPE WORDS

Clues across

STORY WORDS

2 down

11 across

5 down

6 down

10 across

8 across

7 across
(2 words)

1 down

4 across

9 across

12 across

3 down
(2 words)

Harder crosswords

The number in brackets after the clue tells you the number of letters in the answer word.

A

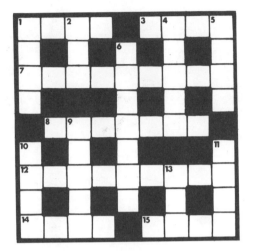

Clues across:
1 The opposite of 'light' (4)
3 Wooden building in the garden (4)
7 The third weekday (9)
8 Game played with glass balls (7)
12 The ninth month (9)
14 The farmer must sow this before his crops will grow (4)
15 Dish of meat and vegetables, sometimes called 'Irish ****' (4)

Clues down:
1 The opposite of 'up' (4)
2 Colours of the Union Jack: ***, white and blue (3)
4 A row of small bushes making a 'fence' round a garden (5)
5 There are seven of them in one week (4)
6 Name for stones found on the sea-shore (7)
9 ''An ***** a day keeps the doctor away'' (5)
10 The girl **** a question (4)
11 A large black British bird (4)
13 A cricketer hits the ball with a *** (3)

B

Clues across:
1 One who plays a game for two teams with ball, bats and wickets (9)
Pretty and healthy (5)
Where cowboys try to ride wild horses and bulls (5)
A bird or a joke (4)
No charge (4)
Old length equal to about 2.5 cm (4)
Day of sporting events (4)
Stretch out for (5)
Pattern on cycle or car tyre (5)
Amuse an audience (9)

Clues down:
2 Type of tube inside a cycle tyre (5)
3 They unlock doors (4)
4 Goes round a wheel (4)
5 One who is on a horse, cycle or motorbike (5)
6 Record of runs and bowling figures at a cricket match (10)
7 Game similar to snooker (9)
12 Olympic athletes run in the 3,000m steeple***** (5)
14 Enclosed area for sports (5)
15 A kick at goal (4)
16 A world class performer or super**** (4)

13

Word detective

Search for little words inside each of these long ones. Keep the letters in the same order.

Look at this example.

mother

moth ___

___ other

___ her

Now try these!

1 teacher

_____

_____

_____

_____

2 postage

_____

_____

_____

_____

3 wearing

_____

_____

_____

4 shopping

_____

_____

_____

5 newspaper

_____

_____

_____

_____

14

Sounds the same

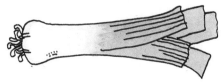

These words sound the same but are spelt differently. Choose the correct word to go with the picture and write it underneath.

1 pair/pear

_____

2 leek/leak

_____

3 flour/flower

_____

4 tail/tale

_____

5 cereal/serial

_____

6 knows/nose

_____

Write the word which sounds the same but has a different spelling.

7 **bare** _____

8 **meet** _____

9 **wood** _____

10 **sun** _____

11 **sale** _____

12 **deer** _____

Animal anagrams

Unscramble the animal names and draw a line to the correct picture. Write the word.

danpa

hdiplon

olaka

matipopusoph

everab

lodorcice

ligorla

genipun

pelroad

orankago

On the farm

Find the words hidden in the square. You can go forwards, backwards, up, down, or diagonally.

chick

horse

pig

hay

lambs

farmer

sack

saddle

goose

pond

sheepdog

sheep

a	c	w	b	d	f	a	r	m	e	r
b	g	o	o	s	e	v	w	x	s	y
f	a	c	q	h	b	y	r	s	a	e
t	u	r	x	e	u	a	w	v	d	k
m	c	r	n	e	l	h	r	f	d	r
s	h	e	e	p	l	h	t	n	l	u
g	i	j	l	d	a	k	o	p	e	t
q	c	v	k	o	m	p	u	r	t	s
z	k	c	y	g	b	i	h	c	s	n
m	a	v	t	z	s	g	v	o	m	e
s	c	a	r	e	c	r	o	w	u	w

bull

turkey

scarecrow

barn

cow

Cooking

Here is a recipe for making gingerbread men. Imagine that you have no ingredients or equipment. Make a list of all the things you will need to buy.

INGREDIENTS

100g plain flour
½ level teaspoonful
    bicarbonate of soda
25g brown sugar
50g margarine
75g golden syrup
1 level teaspoonful
    ground ginger
Currants for
    decoration

EQUIPMENT

Rolling pin
Baking sheet
Mixing bowl
Wooden spoon
Tablespoon
Sieve
Teaspoon
Gingerbread man
    cutter

1 Put oven on at Gas Mark 5 (electricity 375°F/190°C).
2 Cream the margarine and sugar together, add the golden syrup and ground ginger and mix well.
3 Sift in the flour and the bicarbonate of soda. Mix well together.
4 Turn onto a well floured board and work some of the flour into the surface of the dough.
5 Roll out to about 1cm thick and cut out gingerbread man shapes. Add currants for eyes and nose.
6 Bake for 10 – 12 minutes, until golden brown and firm at the edges. (The centre will remain soft until they are cold.)

Make a frog puppet

These pictures show you how to make a frog puppet from a paper plate.

Write the instructions to go with the pictures.

You will need:
paper plate
2 sections from an egg box
2 milk bottle tops
paint and glue

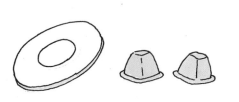

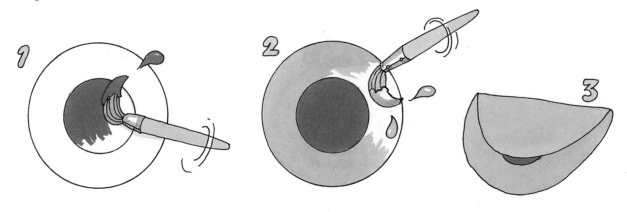

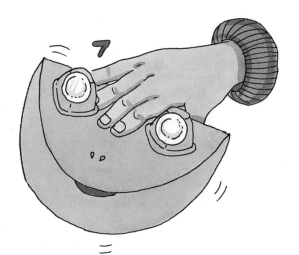

1 _____

2 _____

3 _____

4 _____

5 _____

6 _____

7 _____

Fruit and vegetables

From the jumbled letters below, sort out the names of three fruits. You can only use each letter once.

1 _____

2 _____

3 _____

Write out the names of the fruit and vegetables in the picture.

1 _____
2 _____
3 _____
4 _____
5 _____
6 _____
7 _____
8 _____
9 _____
10 _____

Shopping

ook at the clues in the shop windows and
rite the name of the kind of shop in the space.

Write your own
shopping list of
things you would
like to buy.

SHOPPING LIST

Months of the year

Twelve children each have a birthday in a different month. Count the candles, check the list below and write the name of the **month** on the correct cake.

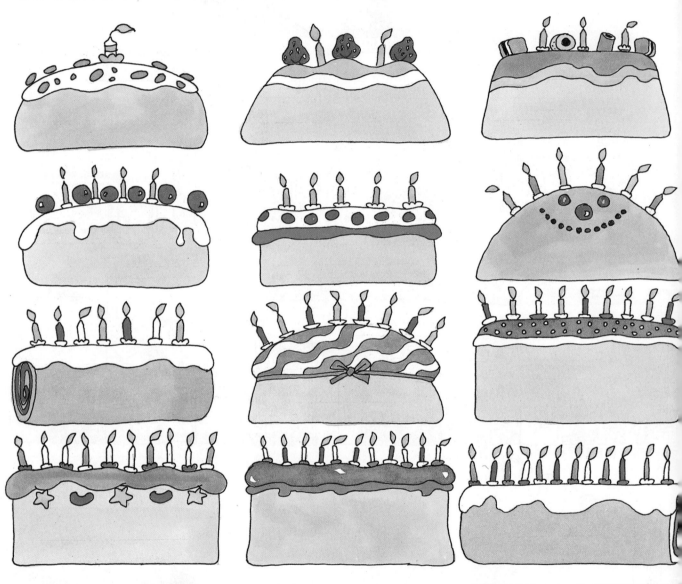

NAME	AGE	MONTH	NAME	AGE	MONTH
John	4	April	Liz	2	February
Sara	10	October	Daniel	6	June
Jim	1	January	Sita	9	September
Ashok	5	May	David	3	March
Kate	8	August	Michelle	11	November
Tom	12	December	Jo	7	July

Numbers

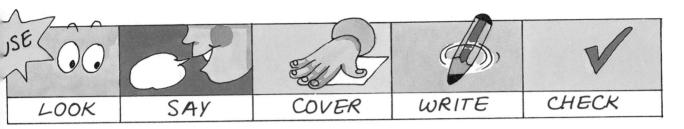

| LOOK | SAY | COVER | WRITE | CHECK |

one 1 _____	eleven 11 _____
two 2 _____	twelve 12 _____
three 3 _____	twenty 20 _____
four 4 _____	thirty 30 _____
five 5 _____	forty 40 _____
six 6 _____	fifty 50 _____
seven 7 _____	hundred 100 _____
eight 8 _____	thousand 1000_____
nine 9 _____	million 1,000,000 _____
ten 10 _____	nought 0 _____

Now write the answers to these questions using number words.

1 Number of days in a week? _____

2 Number of spots on a dice? _____

3 Number of pence in £2.50? _____

4 Number of hours in a day? _____

Give yourself a test!

These words are used often.
Check that you can spell them all.

use   LOOK   SAY   COVER   WRITE   CHECK

he _____   was _____
by _____   with _____
our _____   were _____
of _____   for _____
the _____   my _____
to _____   that _____
went _____   then _____
and _____

have _____
his _____
out _____
some _____
they _____
are _____
go _____
little _____

SCORE

[ ]

one _____   here _____
saw _____   like _____
she _____   make _____
there _____   once _____
this _____   their _____
when _____   away _____
about _____   after _____
because _____ made _____

Well done if you got them all right! You're a good speller!!